Easy Quilting Projects

COMPILED BY **Barbara Delaney**

INTERWEAVE.
interweave.com

*The projects in this collection were
originally published in other Interweave
publications, including* 101 Patchwork,
Modern Patchwork, Quilt Scene,
Quilting Arts, *and* Stitch *magazines.
Some have been altered to update
information and/or conform to space
limitations.*

Interweave
A division of F+W Media, Inc.
201 East Fourth Street
Loveland, CO 80537
interweave.com

Manufactured in the United States
by Versa Press

ISBN 978-1-62033-556-7 (pbk.)

Contents

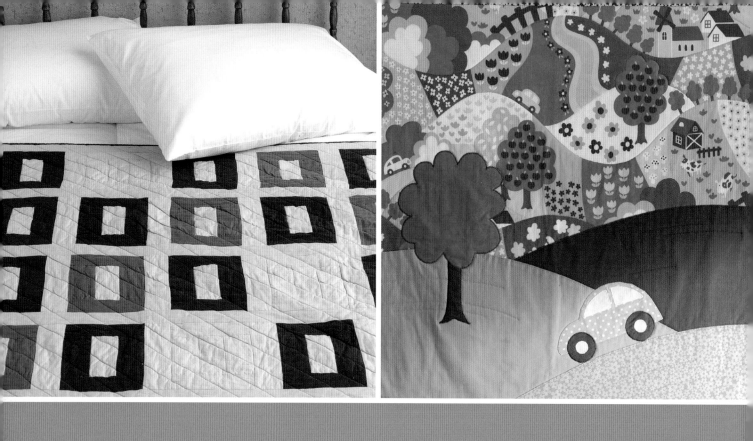

Creative Quilts

Nine Patch Rearranged

BY VIVIKA HANSEN DENEGRE

I delight in the variety of beautiful ways that new fabric collections are packaged. Jelly rolls? I have them at the ready for strip quilts and quick projects. Fat quarters? They are tucked into baskets in my studio. But what about the 10" squares from Moda's Layer Cake packs? I used one package for the featured quilt! Machine quilted by Saima Davis.

Materials

☐ Coordinating print fabrics, 40 squares 10" × 10" (25.5 × 25.5 cm)

☐ Solid fabric, 5 squares 10" × 10" (25.5 × 25.5 cm; I used ¾ yd [68.5 cm] of a bright pink solid.)

☐ Backing fabric, 3¾ yd (3.4 m)

☐ Binding fabric, ¾ yd (68.5 cm)

☐ Batting, 62" × 76" (157.5 × 193 cm; or twin size)

Finished Size

57" × 71" (145 × 180.5 cm)

Directions

The blocks for this quilt are made using a really fun and simple piecing technique. Starting with 10" (25.5 cm) squares I made huge nine-patch blocks, each with a solid pink center square. Then I cut each nine patch into quarters. The resulting blocks were rearranged into a 4 × 5 grid and sewn together to make the quilt top, hence the title "Nine Patch Rearranged." I learned this technique from a quilting friend, using much smaller nine patches. I have heard it referred to as "Disappearing Nine Patch" and "Split Nine Patch."

1 For the first oversized nine-patch block, select nine 10" (25.5 cm) squares (you'll need 8 print squares and 1 solid square). On a design wall or other flat surface, arrange the squares into 3 rows of 3, with the solid square in the middle.

 Tip

+ Place the fabrics you want to dominate your quilt in the 4 corner positions, and those that will be less dominant in the middle row positions.

2 To piece the oversized nine-patch block, first sew the squares into 3 rows. Press the seams to 1 side, pressing in the opposite direction for the center row. Sew the 3 rows together. Press these seams toward the center, then press the block and set it aside.

Repeat the process, making a total of 5 blocks.

3 Cut the blocks into quarters by cutting in half from top to bottom, then side to side.

4 Using a design wall, arrange the blocks into 5 rows of 4 blocks each. Play with the placement of the colors, and rearrange the blocks to your heart's content.

5 Sew the rows, pressing the seams in opposite directions, and then sew the rows together, nesting the seams for matching corners. Press the entire quilt top.

6 To prepare the backing, cut the backing fabric in half from selvedge to selvedge to get 2 pieces about 67" (170 cm) × WOF (width of fabric). Sew these pieces together along a 67" (170 cm) edge.

7 Layer the quilt top with the batting and backing. Quilt and bind as desired. The featured quilt was quilted with an overall spiral design.

 Tip

+ Because of the large size of the nine-patch blocks, it is easiest to locate the center by measuring 4¾" (12 cm) from the side seams of the middle row.

VIVIKA HANSEN DENEGRE is the editor of *Quilting Arts Magazine*. Check out her blog at quiltingdaily.com.

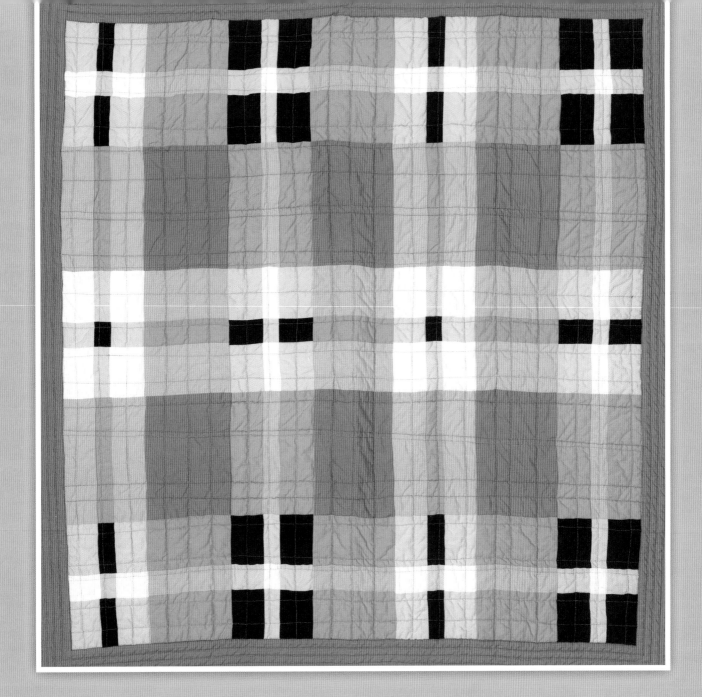

Work Shirt Quilt

BY REBECCA ROACH

This is an easy quilt that's perfect for the little boys in your life! Using six solid fabrics, you can whip up this project in a weekend. Make this quilt in someone's favorite colors and it's a perfect gift for any guy on your list—no matter his age.

Materials

- ☐ ¼ yd (23 cm) white fabric cut into:
    - —two 2½" × 44" (6.5 × 112 cm) strips
    - —one 1½" × 44" (3.8 × 112 cm) strip
- ☐ ½ yd (46 cm) light gray fabric cut into:
    - —two 2½" × 44" (6.5 × 112 cm) strips
    - —one 1½" × 44" (3.8 × 112 cm) strip
    - —six 5½" × 2" (14 × 5 cm) rectangles
    - —six 5½" × 3½" (14 × 9 cm) rectangles
- ☐ ½ yd (46 cm) light blue fabric cut into:
    - —four 2½" × 44" (6.5 × 112 cm) strips
    - —two 1½" × 44" (3.8 × 112 cm) strips
- ☐ ½ yd (46 cm) medium blue fabric cut into:
    - —two 2½" × 44" (6.5 × 112 cm) strips
    - —one 1½" × 44" (3.8 × 112 cm) strip
    - —three 5½" × 2" (14 × 5 cm) rectangles
    - —twelve 5½" × 3½" (14 × 9 cm) rectangles
- ☐ ¼ yd (23 cm) dark blue fabric cut into:
    - —two 2½" × 44" (6.5 × 112 cm) strips
    - —one 1½" × 44" (3.8 × 112 cm) strip
- ☐ ¾ yd (68.5 cm) bright orange fabric cut into:
    - —four 2½" × 44" (6.5 × 112 cm) strips
    - —six 5½" × 8" (14 × 20.5 cm) rectangles

Finished Size

39" × 42" (99 × 106.5 cm)

Directions

1 Begin by sewing a 2½" (6.5 cm) strip of medium blue fabric to both sides of the 1½" (3.8 cm) strip of gray fabric.

2 Take this new strip set to your cutting mat and cut it into 4 blocks measuring 8" (20.5 cm) long.

3 Next, sew a 2½" (6.5 cm) strip of gray fabric to both sides of the 1½" (3.8 cm) strip of medium blue fabric.

4 Take this strip set to your cutting mat and cut it into 4 blocks measuring 8" (20.5 cm) long. You're now finished with all of the horizontal striped blocks!

5 Sew a 2½" (6.5 cm) strip of dark blue fabric to both sides of a 1½" (3.8 cm) strip of light blue fabric.

6 Take this strip set to your cutting mat and cut it into 8 units measuring 3½" (9 cm) long and 2 units measuring 2" (5 cm) long.

7 Repeat steps 5 and 6 using 2 light blue 2½" (6.5 cm) strips and 1 dark blue 1½" (3.8 cm) strip.

8 Sew a 2½" (6.5 cm) strip of light blue fabric to both sides of the 1½" (3.8 cm) strip of white fabric.

9 Take this strip set to your cutting mat and cut it into 4 units measuring 3½" (9 cm) long and 4 units measuring 2" (5 cm) long.

10 Sew a 2½" (6.5 cm) strip of white fabric to both sides of a 1½" (3.8 cm) strip of light blue fabric.

11 Take this strip set to your cutting mat and cut it into 4 units measuring 3½" (9 cm) long and 4 units measuring 2" (5 cm) long.

12 Now, use the units you've just cut to begin creating 9-patch blocks. Sew a 3½" (9 cm) dark blue/light blue/dark blue unit to both sides of a 2" (5 cm) light blue/white/light blue unit. Repeat until you have 4 blocks.

13 Sew a 3½" (9 cm) light blue/dark blue/light blue unit to both sides of a 2" (5 cm) white/light blue/white unit. Repeat until you have 4 blocks.

14 Next, sew a 3½" (9 cm) light blue/white/light blue unit to both sides of a 2" (5 cm) dark blue/light blue/dark blue unit. Repeat to create 2 identical blocks.

15 Finally, sew a 3½" (9 cm) white/light blue/white unit to both sides of a 2" (5 cm) light blue/dark blue/light blue unit. Repeat to create 2 identical blocks. You've finished all the 9-patch blocks!

16 To create the vertical stripe blocks, sew a 5½" × 3½" (14 × 9 cm) medium blue rectangle unit to both sides of a 5½" × 2" (14 × 5 cm) gray rectangle unit. Repeat until you have 6 identical blocks.

17 Next, sew a 5½" × 3½" (14 × 9 cm) gray rectangle unit to both sides of a 5½" × 2" (14 × 5 cm) medium blue unit. Repeat until you have 3 identical blocks.

18 All 35 blocks are now done! Sew them together according to the diagram.

19 Use the remaining 2½" (6.5 cm) strips of orange fabric to create a border. Sew a strip to both sides of the quilt top and use a rotary cutter to trim away the extra length. Finally, sew the other 2 strips to the top and bottom and trim.

20 Quilt and bind as desired. Enjoy! 🌿

- -

REBECCA ROACH has been a quilter since 2004. She design patterns and fabric designs. Visit her online at frybreadquilts.wordpress.com.

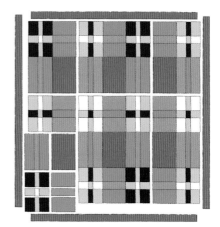

diagram

Woven Stripes Quilt

BY CAROL ZENTGRAF

This fun and funky quilt is easy to make. A perfect project for the beginner sewer, it will look anything but simple when it's complete. Choose your favorite colors and make a statement. Whether you go with big and bold stripes, soft pastels, or a combination, this quilt will brighten up any room.

Materials

☐ ⅜ yd (34.5 cm) each of 11 different striped cotton fabrics for quilt blocks (shown: stripes from Michael Miller Fabrics)

☐ 4 yd (3.6 m) of striped cotton fabric for quilt backing

☐ 1 yd (91.5 cm) of striped cotton fabric for bias binding

☐ 60" × 70" (152.5 × 178 cm) low-loft batting

☐ Coordinating sewing thread for piecing and quilting

☐ Bent-arm (quilting) safety pins

☐ Walking foot attachment for sewing machine

☐ Rotary cutter, rigid acrylic ruler, and self-healing mat

☐ Pencil

☐ Masking or painter's tape (for labeling fabric blocks)

Finished Size

50" × 60" (127 × 152.5 cm)

Notes

✳ All seam allowances are ¼" (6 mm) unless otherwise noted. Sew seams with right sides together.

✳ For explanations of terms and techniques, see Sewing Basics.

Cut the Fabric

1 Cut the following pieces as directed, using a rotary cutter, rigid acrylic ruler, and self-healing mat. Assign each fabric a number and use a pencil and masking or painter's tape to label each piece with the fabric number. This will help avoid confusion as you sew the blocks together.

From the striped block fabrics, cut the following pieces:

—From each of eight fabrics cut three 10½" (26.5 cm) squares for quilt blocks.

—From each of the three remaining fabrics cut two 10½" (26.5 cm) squares for quilt blocks.

From the fabric for the backing, cut:

—Two 31" × 70" (79 × 178 cm) rectangles.

From the fabric for the binding, cut:

—2¼" (5.5 cm) wide bias strips to total 6½ yd (5.9 m). Refer to Cutting Bias Strips in Sewing Basics.

Piece the Quilt Top

2 Referring to the assembly diagram, arrange the 30 fabric blocks in six rows of five blocks each.

3 Beginning with the top row, sew the blocks together. Press the seam allowances to one side. Repeat to sew each row of blocks, and for each row, alternate the direction in which you press the seam allowances. (For example, press the seam allowances in the top row to the right, the second row to the left, the third row to the right, etc.) This ensures neat corners when the rows are sewn together.

4 Pin the first and second rows together, matching the seams. Sew the rows together. Be sure that you don't accidentally sew the rows together out of order. Press the seam allowance in one direction.

5 Follow the process in step 4 to sew the third row to the second row, pressing in the same direction. Join the remaining rows in the same manner.

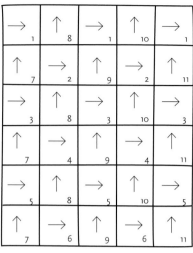

Assembly Diagram

Assemble the Quilt

6 Sew the long edges of the two backing rectangles together. Press the seam open.

7 Place the backing right-side down on a large flat surface. Center the batting on top of the backing, smoothing out the layers so that they lie flat and un-wrinkled. Place the quilt top right-side up on top of the batting and backing, again smoothing out the layers.

8 Beginning in the center of the quilt top and working toward the outside edges, pin the layers together with quilt-ing safety pins spaced about 4"–6" (10.5–15 cm) apart. Next, pin around the outside edge of the quilt top.

9 Install the walking foot on your ma-chine, and then sew the layers togeth-er, stitching in the ditch or following a design of your choosing. Backtack at the beginning and end of each stitch line, and remove the pins as needed. Stitch around the outside edges of the quilt top, within the ¼" (6 mm) seam allowance.

10 Trim off the excess batting and back-ing fabric to match the quilt top and square up the corners of the quilt.

Finishing

11 Sew the short ends of the binding strips together with diagonal seams to create a single strip, referring to Create Binding in Sewing Basics. Fold the assembled strip in half lengthwise with wrong sides together and press to create double-layer binding.

12 Sew the binding to the quilt, follow-ing the directions under Binding with Mitered Corners (option B) in Sewing Basics.

- -

CAROL ZENTGRAF is a writer, designer, and editor specializing in sewing, embroidery, textiles, painting, and decorating. She designs for several magazines and fabric company websites. Carol is also the author of seven home décor sewing books.

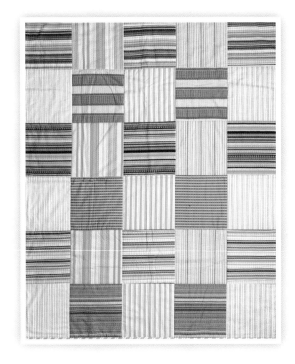

Materials

- ☐ Thirty 4½" × 12½" (11.5 × 31.5 cm) strips of assorted fabric

- ☐ Forty 3½" × 12½" (9 × 31.5 cm) strips of assorted fabric

- ☐ Batting, throw size

- ☐ Backing fabric (I used large scraps and pieced them together to make a 48½" × 60½" [123 × 153.5 cm] rectangle.)

Finished Size

48" × 60" (122 × 152.5 cm)

Scrappy Patchwork Quilt

BY LINDSEY MURRAY MCCLELLAND

This scrappy lap quilt is a great way to use up large scraps from your stash! Because this is a scrap quilt, there is no exact pattern to follow. Simply use coordinating fabrics from your stash to create a funky, fun look. And to keep this project quick and easy, you can use a pillowcase finish like I did, if you wish.

Directions

1. Piece 10 blocks using three 4½" × 12½" (11.5 × 31.5 cm) strips each.

2. Piece 10 blocks using four 3½" × 12½" (9 × 31.5 cm) strips each. (All 20 blocks should measure 12½" × 12½" [31.5 × 31.5 cm] square.)

3. Lay out the blocks in a pleasing fashion, making 5 rows of 4 blocks each.

4. When you are satisfied with the arrangement, sew the blocks together in rows, and then sew the rows together.

Tip

+ Rotate the blocks to create more interest.

5. Piece the backing fabric if necessary. The back of my quilt is shown below.

6. Baste the quilt top to the batting. Then layer the backing fabric on the quilt top, right sides together. Trim all of the edges even, trimming through all 3 layers. Sew around the edge of the quilt, leaving a 6" (15 cm) opening on 1 side.

7. Clip the corners close to the seam.

8. Turn the quilt right-side out, and whip-stitch the opening closed.

9. Quilt as desired. I used a simple grid of zigzag stitching. 🍃

LINDSEY MURRAY MCCLELLAND is the former assistant editor of *Modern Patchwork, Studios,* and *Quilting Arts In Stitches.* She enjoys spending time in her studio quilting and never turns down the opportunity to read a good book. Lindsey lives in Stow, Massachusetts with her husband, two dogs, and cat.

Cool Waters Lap Quilt

BY KEVIN KOSBAB

This simple quilt is all about contrast: a sunny orange center plays off a border of cool aqua shades, while hard-edged piecing contrasts with free-form quilting. The construction couldn't be easier, and the scribbly quilting style is an imperfectionist's dream.

Materials

Note: All fabrics are 45" (114.5 cm) wide cotton unless otherwise noted.

☐ 1⅓ yd (1.2 mm) of solid cotton fabric for center (shown: orange)

☐ 16 assorted scraps of 3–16 different solid fabrics in a single color range, each at least 9" × 9" (23 × 23 cm), for border (shown: shades of blue-green)

☐ 6 assorted scraps of 3–6 different print fabrics in the same color range, each at least 9" × 9" (23 × 23 cm), for border (shown: aqua polka dots, geometric print, and birds print)

☐ 3 yd (2.7 m) of fabric for backing (shown: dark aqua squares print)

☐ ½ yd (46 cm) of fabric for binding (shown: orange polka dot)

☐ 54" × 64" (137 × 162.5 cm) piece of batting

☐ Coordinating sewing thread

☐ Quilting thread in coordinating colors (shown: aqua and orange)

☐ Bent-arm safety pins or quilt-basting spray

☐ Water-soluble fabric-marking pen (optional)

☐ Rotary cutter, rigid acrylic ruler, and self-healing mat

☐ Darning or free-motion foot for sewing machine

Finished Size

51½" × 60" (131 × 152.5 cm)

Notes

✳ All seam allowances are ¼" (6 mm) unless otherwise noted.

✳ For explanations of terms and techniques, see Sewing Basics.

✳ Try other freehand quilting designs in the center panel or use the open space to quilt a representational motif.

Cut the Front Fabric

1 Cut the following pieces as directed.

—One 34½" × 43" (87.5 × 109 cm) rectangle from the center fabric

—One or more 9" × 9" (23 × 23 cm) squares from each of the solid border fabrics, for a total of 16 squares

—One or more 9" × 9" (23 × 23 cm) squares from each of the print border fabrics, for a total of 6 squares

—Six 2" (5 cm) × width of fabric strips from the binding fabric

Piece the Borders

2 On a design wall or your work surface, arrange the border squares around the center panel, distributing the prints throughout the border. Arrange 5 squares for each side border, 4 squares each for the top and bottom, and 4 squares for the corners.

3 When you're satisfied with the arrangement, assemble the 5 left-side border squares into a strip, sewing each seam with right sides together. Press the seam allowances to one side. Repeat to join the 5 right-side border squares into a strip. Join the 4 top border squares and the adjacent corners into a strip; repeat to assemble the bottom border and corner squares. Press the seam allowances to one side, pressing the outermost seam allowances away from the corner.

Assemble the Quilt Top

4 Pin the side border strips to the center panel with right sides together. Sew both border strips to the center and press the seam allowances outward, toward the border.

5 Pin the top and bottom border strips to the center panel, right sides together, aligning the side border seams with the outermost seams of the top and bottom border strips. Sew both border strips to the quilt top and press the seam allowances outward (refer to the diagram on page 16 to see the arrangement of the quilt top pieces).

Prepare for Quilting

6 Use a water-soluble fabric marking pen to do any marking necessary for quilting placement. The sample was free-motion quilted freehand, marking only the basic lines on the border and ellipses on the center panel; refer to the diagram on page 16.

7 Cut the backing fabric into two 1½ yd (1.4 m) pieces and remove the selvedges. Pin the 2 pieces, right sides together, along a 54" (137 cm) edge, sew, and press the seam allowance open. Trim the rectangle parallel to the seam to make a 54" × 64" (137 × 162.5 cm) backing.

8 With the backing wrong-side up, center the batting on the backing, then center the assembled quilt top right-side up to create a quilt sandwich. Baste the three layers together with safety pins or basting spray. If using safety pins, pin in rows, spacing pins no more than 6" (15 cm) apart.

Construction Diagram

Quilting and Finishing

Refer to the diagram above for
assistance with the following steps.

9 Set up your sewing machine for free-
motion quilting, dropping or covering
the feed dogs and installing a darning or free-motion foot; check your
instruction manual for details. The
sample uses a meandering freehand
quilting style to contrast with the
geometric piecing. With contrasting
thread, quilt a line parallel to the side
edges through the center panel from
the center of one top-border square
to the center of the corresponding
bottom-border square, interrupting
the line periodically with an ellipse. To
quilt the ellipses, sew two complete
passes all the way around, roughly
following the same outline, then sew
another half pass to get to the other
side of the ellipse and continue the
straight line. Vary the ellipse sizes.

10 Using thread matching the center
panel, quilt meandering lines in the
center panel to fill the space between
the lines and ellipses from the previous step.

11 Using thread matching the border
color tones, quilt a rough square in the
center of each border square and a line
connecting the squares, following the
technique described for the ellipses in
Step 9.

12 Remove the selvedges from the binding strips and join them with diagonal
seams (see Sewing Basics) to create
a strip at least 185" (4.7 m) long. Fold
the strip in half lengthwise, with wrong
sides together, and press to create
double-layer binding.

13 Bind the quilt's outer edges, following the instructions for option B
under Binding with Mitered Corners
in Sewing Basics. In the sample quilt,
the back of the binding was secured
by stitching in the ditch from the front
rather than slip-stitching the binding
by hand. 🌿

- - - - - - - - - - - - - - - - - - - -

KEVIN KOSBAB is a freelance writer,
an editor, and a pattern designer.
Find his Feed Dog Designs patterns in
stores and on the Web at feeddog.net.

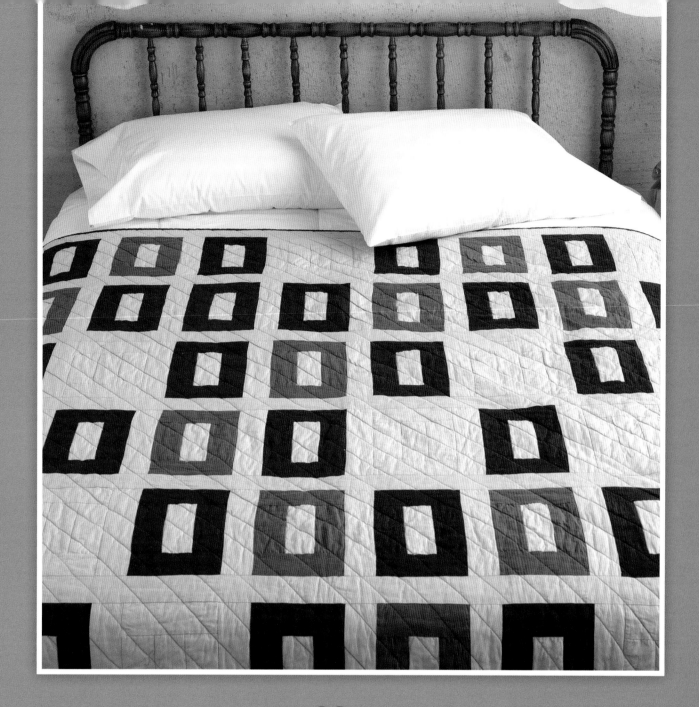

Dare-to-Be Different Quilt

BY KARRIE WINTERS

Using a modern palette, create a simple quilt that uses strip piecing and straight line quilting for a quick finish. Featuring one contrasting block, the design is inspired by one of life's lessons—to follow your own path and be your own person.

Materials

Note: All fabric is 44" (112 cm) wide cotton. Kona Cotton Solids by Robert Kaufman were used here. Use similar fabrics to those listed or use desired colors/ prints. The first three listings should be different hues of the same color; the last two listings should be two contrasting colors.

☐ ⅝ yd (57 cm) of a light-hue solid (A; shown: light purple [Thistle])

☐ 1 yd (91.5 cm) of a medium-hue solid (B; shown: medium purple [Crocus])

☐ 7¼ yd (6.6 m) of a dark-hue solid (C; 2 yd [1.8 m] used for blocks and binding; 5¼ yd [4.8 m] used for backing; shown: dark purple [Hibiscus])

☐ ⅛ yd (11.5 cm) of a contrast solid (D; shown: red [Rich Red])

☐ 3 yd (2.7 m) of another contrast solid (E; shown: gray [Ash])

☐ 75" × 83" (190.5 × 211 cm) piece of batting

☐ Cotton thread for piecing and quilting

☐ Bent-arm safety pins or quilt-basting spray

☐ Rotary cutter, rigid acrylic ruler, and self-healing mat (optional, for cutting)

☐ Walking foot with a quilting guide for sewing machine to quilt and to sew on the binding

Finished Size

67" × 75" (170 × 190.5 cm)

Notes

* All seam allowances are ¼" (6 mm) unless otherwise noted. Sew pieces with right sides together.

* For explanations of terms and techniques, see Sewing Basics.

* To prevent later shrinkage or bleeding, prewash and dry all fabric before cutting using the same method you intend to use for the finished quilt. Alternatively, wash the quilt after finishing it to give it a soft, lived-in look.

* The abbreviation "WOF" refers to "width of fabric," which means to cut selvedge to selvedge. Cut off the selvedges before using any strip cut across the width of the fabric.

* Assign letters to each fabric as indicated in the fabric list. You may want to write a list of each color and the letter it is assigned and then keep your fabric strips in piles by color while following the instructions. This will make organization easier.

* The term "subcut" in the instructions simply refers to cutting pieces you have already cut into smaller pieces.

* "Sashing" is the term used for borders between quilt blocks.

Cut the Fabric

1 From fabric A, cut:

—7 strips that measure 2½" (6.5 cm) × WOF. Set aside 5 strips and subcut the remaining 3 strips into 18 pieces measuring 6½" × 2½" (16.5 × 6.5 cm).

From fabric B, cut:

—11 strips that measure 2½" (6.5 cm) × WOF. Set aside 6 strips and subcut the remaining 5 strips into 28 pieces measuring 6½" × 2½" (16.5 × 6.5 cm).

From fabric C, cut:

—24 strips that measure 2½" (6.5 cm) × WOF. Set aside 16 strips (8 of these strips will be used for binding) and subcut the remaining 8 strips into 48 pieces measuring 6½" × 2½" (16.5 × 6.5 cm).

From fabric D, cut:

—1 strip that measures 2½" (6.5 cm) × WOF. Subcut this strip into 4 pieces measuring 6½" × 2½" (16.5 × 6.5 cm).

From fabric E, cut the following pieces as directed.

—Blocks: Cut 10 strips that measure 2½" (6.5 cm) × WOF. Cut another piece that measures 6½" × 2½" (16.5 × 6.5 cm) to make the contrast block.

—Sashing: Cut 11 strips that are 2½" (6.5 cm) × WOF. Subcut these into 42 pieces measuring 2½" × 10½" (6.5 × 26.6 cm) for vertical sashing. Cut 10 more strips that are 2½" (6.5 cm) × WOF for horizontal sashing.

—Border: Cut 8 strips that measure 2½" (6.5 cm) × WOF.

Sew the Blocks

2 Sew a long edge of a fabric A WOF strip to the long edge of a fabric E WOF strip. Sew another fabric A strip to the remaining long edge of the fabric E strip. Press the seam allowances toward fabric A. Repeat the entire step to make another 3-strip set.

3 Subcut the strip sets from Step 6 into 9 pieces measuring 6½" × 6½" (16.5 × 16.5 cm (**FIGURE 1**).

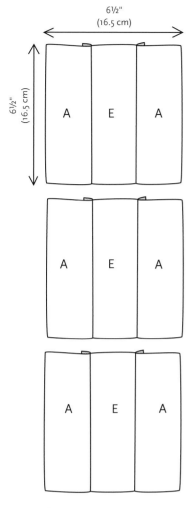

6½" (16.5 cm)

6½" (16.5 cm)

figure 1

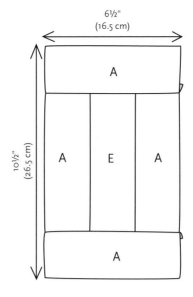

6½" (16.5 cm)

10½" (26.5 cm)

figure 2

4 Sew a 6½" × 2½" (16.5 × 6.5 cm) fabric A strip to each end of one of the strip sets just cut, perpendicular to the existing seam lines, creating a block that measures 6½" × 10½" (16.5 × 26.5 cm; **FIGURE 2**). Repeat with each strip set for a total of 9 blocks.

5 Using fabric B strips instead of fabric A, repeat Step 2 to make three 3-strip sets. Subcut them into 14 pieces as described in Step 3, then add strips of fabric B to the ends as described in Step 4 to make a total of 14 blocks.

6 Using fabric C strips instead of fabric A, repeat Step 2 to make four 3-strip sets. Subcut them into 24 pieces as described in Step 3, then add strips of fabric C to the ends as described in Step 4 to make a total of 24 blocks.

7 Sew a long edge of a 6½" × 2½" (16.5 × 6.5 cm) fabric D piece to the long edge

of the 6½" × 2½" (16.5 × 6.5 cm) fabric E piece. Sew another 6½" × 2½" (16.5 × 6.5 cm) fabric D piece to the remaining long edge of the fabric E piece. Press the seam allowances toward fabric D. Add strips of fabric D to each end as described in Step 4.

Assemble the Quilt

8 Arrange the blocks according to the construction diagram on page 20, laying out six 8-block rows.

9 Sew a 6½" × 2½" (16.5 × 6.5 cm) sashing piece to the right-hand side of the first 7 blocks in each row. Do not add sashing to the blocks in the rightmost column. Press the seam allowances in one direction.

10 Sew the 8 blocks of the first row together, being sure to keep the unsashed block at the right end of the row. Press the seam allowances in one direction. Repeat to sew the blocks of each of the remaining 6 rows together.

11 Sew the 10 fabric E strips that were cut for the horizontal sashing into sets of two, end to end, to create 5 strips measuring 2½" (6.5 cm) × about 84" (213.5 cm).

12 Pin one of these strips to the bottom of each of rows 1–5. The sashing strip will be longer than the row; trim the ends flush with the row. Sew the

sashing to each row and press the seam allowances in one direction.

13 Carefully aligning the blocks, pin and sew row 1 to row 2 along the adjacent edges, then to row 3, etc., until all rows are assembled, being sure to keep the unsashed row at the bottom.

14 To add the borders, sew the 8 border strips of fabric E into sets of two, end to end, creating 4 strips measuring 2½" (6.5 cm) × about 84" (213.5 cm). Pin and sew a border piece to the right and left side of the quilt top. Trim the ends of the borders flush with the quilt top and press the seam allowances toward the borders. Pin and sew the remaining border pieces to the top and bottom of the quilt top, trim, and press. Gently press the quilt top flat.

15 Piece a quilt backing from fabric C to 75" × 83" (190.5 × 211 cm). To make a solid backing, cut two 37¾" × 83" (93.5 × 211 cm) rectangles from fabric C, sew them together along one of the long sides, and press the seam allowance open. To make a pieced backing with blocks as seen on the sample, make three more 6½" × 10½" (16.5 × 26.5 cm) blocks using scraps left from the front blocks. Cut 3 strips measuring 10½" × 69½" (26.5 × 176.5 cm) from fabric C. Referring to the photo on page 17, subcut one of the strips parallel to the short ends and insert one of the back blocks between the resulting pieces, sewing each cut edge to one long side of the block, then do the same for the remaining strips and back blocks, staggering the subcut so the blocks line up on the diagonal as shown. Cut a strip measuring 10½" × 75" (26.5 × 190.5 cm) and a rectangle measuring 43" × 75" (109 × 190.5 cm) from fabric C and sew each to one of the long sides of the pieced strips. If necessary, seam smaller pieces of fabric C together to achieve these sizes.

16 With the backing wrong-side up, center the batting on top, then center the quilt top right-side up to create a quilt sandwich. Baste the three layers together with safety pins or basting spray. If using safety pins, pin in rows, spacing pins no more than 6" (15 cm) apart.

1

2

3

4

5

6

Construction Diagram

Quilt and Finish

17 With coordinating thread and a walking foot on your sewing machine, quilt as desired. The sample quilt was quilted with straight stitches placed diagonally from corner to corner with a spacing of 2" (5 cm) between lines. A quilting guide helps keep the spacing even without marking.

18 Square up the quilt and trim the excess batting and backing to match the quilt top. Using the 8 fabric C binding strips cut earlier, seam the strips end to end into a continuous length with diagonal

seams and create double-layer binding following the instructions in Sewing Basics. Follow the instructions under Binding with Mitered Corners (option A) in Sewing Basics to bind the edges of the quilt.

19 Wash the quilt to soften it.

- - - - - - - - - - - - - - - - - - - -

KARRIE WINTERS is an avid quilter who loves to teach others. She has patterns with tutorials featured on modabakeshop.com, swatchandstitch .com, and rileyblakedesigns.com. She also blogs at freckledwhimsy.com.

Hilltop Drive Baby Quilt

BY KEVIN KOSBAB

This is the perfect gift for a toddler ready to move into his "big boy" room! With rolling hills and fusible appliqué inspired by a fun landscape print, this baby quilt can quickly come together in a weekend.

Materials

Note; All fabrics are 45" (115 cm) wide cotton unless otherwise noted. Use similar fabrics to those listed or use desired colors/prints.

- ☐ ½ yd (46 cm) green (A) for hill
- ☐ ¼ yd (23 cm) cerulean blue (B) for hill
- ☐ ⅓ yd (30.5 cm) brown (C) for hill and tree trunk
- ☐ ½ yd (46 cm) coordinating floral print for hill (D; shown: blue/green floral)
- ☐ ½ yd (46 cm) landscape print for background (E)
- ☐ 8" × 8" (20.5 × 20.5 cm) scrap cornflower blue for tree leaves (F)
- ☐ 5" × 3" (12.5 × 7.5 cm) scrap white for car windows and hubcaps (G)
- ☐ 8" × 4" (20.5 × 10 cm) scrap aqua polka-dot print for car (H)
- ☐ 1 yd (91.5 cm) backing fabric (shown: coordinating car print)
- ☐ ¼ yd (23 cm) blue/brown floral print for binding

Note: Don't worry if you can't find a similar landscape print—a cloud print would work, too. A coordinating car print was used for the backing to have a more urban look to contrast with the countryside theme of the front.

- ☐ Freezer paper
- ☐ Spray starch (optional)
- ☐ ½ yd (46 cm) lightweight fusible web
- ☐ Sewing or embroidery thread to coordinate with each fabric
- ☐ 1 yd (91 cm) low-loft cotton batting
- ☐ Invisible monofilament thread (optional)
- ☐ Safety pins (recommended: bent-arm quilting safety pins) or quilt-basting spray
- ☐ Walking foot for sewing machine (optional)
- ☐ Baby Car Quilt templates on pages 24 and 25

Finished Size

28" × 33" (71 × 84 cm)

Notes

* All seam allowances are ¼" (6 mm) unless otherwise noted.

* For explanations of terms and techniques, see Sewing Basics.

* If your sewing machine is capable of a blanket stitch, feel free to use that for the appliqué instead of a zigzag stitch.

Make Hill Templates

1. The shapes for each hill are indicated on the provided composite hill template. Trace the 3 straight sides and curve of the A hill template onto the paper (non-waxy) side of freezer paper. Cut the template out around the outer edge and label it. Repeat to make a template for the B hill.

2. The C and D hills face the other direction, so flip the template sheet over and use a light box or a window to trace freezer-paper templates for the C and D hills.

Make Hills

3. Lay each template, shiny side up, on the wrong side of the corresponding fabric, being sure to leave at least a ½" (1.3 cm) margin around the template. Pin each template to the corresponding fabric (A–D), around the perimeter of the template. If the freezer paper curls, anchor it flat with pattern weights or other heavy objects.

4. Cut the curve for each hill ⅜" (1 cm) outside the template edge. Cut the straight sides along the template edge. Do not remove the freezer-paper templates from the fabric.

5. Using the tip of a hot, dry iron, press the seam allowance over the freezer-paper template, making sure the fabric folds tightly around the edge of the template. Clip into the seam allowance along the curved edge every 1"–2" (2.5–5 cm), if necessary, so the seam allowance lies flat against the freezer paper and the fold creates a smooth curve. The shiny side of the freezer paper will hold the turned-under seam allowance in place. Remove the template when the hill fabric has cooled. Use spray starch, if necessary, to hold the pressed seam allowances in place when the template is removed.

Attach Hills

6. Cut a 28" × 17½" (71 × 44.5 cm) rectangle from the landscape print.

7. Referring to the photo at right for placement guidance, arrange the hills and the landscape rectangle as follows. Place the C hill first, aligning the straight right-hand edges and positioning the top of the hill 13" (33 cm) below the top of the landscape rectangle. Pin the hill's curved edge in place, then position the remaining hills in the same way, placing the A hill 16¼" (41.5 cm) from the top of the landscape rectangle, the D hill 7½" (19 cm) from the top of the C hill, and the B hill 8½" (21.5 cm) from the top of the A hill. Make sure the pieces align correctly at the sides and lower edge and that the sides are perpendicular to the top edge. The pinned quilt top should measure 28" × 33" (71 × 84 cm). Make sure each hill has enough overlap to be sewn down along its pressed edge, then pin again so the entire quilt top is securely held together.

8. Starting with the C hill and working your way to the B hill, topstitch each hill in place, ⅛" (3 mm) from the pressed edge, removing the pins as you go. Where a lower hill overlaps the edge being stitched, temporarily fold the upper-layer hill back so it isn't caught in the current seam. Optional: After sewing each hill, flip the quilt top over and trim away the excess fabric of the previous hill, leaving a ¼" (6 mm) seam allowance.

Prepare Appliqués

9. Trace each separate shape from the provided Car and Tree templates onto the paper side of fusible web, leaving at least ½" (1.3 cm) between the shapes.

10. Roughly cut each shape about ¼" (6 mm) outside the traced line. Optional: To reduce stiffness, cut the center out of the fusible shape, leaving a ¼" (6 mm) margin of fusible web inside the line.

11 Following the manufacturer's instructions, press the fusible-web shapes onto the wrong sides of the corresponding (or desired) fabrics as follows. Press the tree trunk and car tires onto fabric C, the tree leaves onto fabric F, the car windows and hubcaps onto fabric G, and the car body onto fabric H.

12 When cool, cut out each fused shape directly on the traced line. Referring to the templates for placement, peel off the paper backing and fuse the windows to the car body and the hubcaps to the tires. Make sure the car body and tires are still backed with paper so they don't stick to the pressing surface.

Appliqué

13 Using a zigzag stitch 2.0 mm wide and 0.3–0.4 mm long, sew the car window and hubcaps to the car body and tires with white thread. The right swing of the needle should fall into the foundation fabric immediately beside the appliqué, while the main body of the stitches falls on the appliqué itself. Pivot frequently with the needle in the foundation fabric for smooth curves. When you have sewn all the way around the shapes, pull the thread ends to the back and knot them.

14 Peel the paper backing off the remaining appliqué shapes (including the car body and tires). Arrange them on the quilt top, referring to the photo above for placement or placing them as desired. When you're satisfied, fuse the appliqués in place, being sure to fuse the car body before the wheels.

15 Matching thread color to the appliqué piece, zigzag stitch around the edges of each appliqué as described in Step 13.

Quilt and Finish

16 Square up the edges of the completed quilt top, if necessary.

17 Cut the backing fabric 33" (84 cm) wide × 36" (91 cm) long. Cut the batting 32" (81 cm) wide × 35" (89 cm) long. With the backing wrong-side up, center the batting on top, then center the quilt top right-side up on the batting to create a quilt "sandwich." Baste the 3 layers together with safety pins or basting spray.

18 With matching or invisible thread and a straight stitch 2.5–3.0 mm long, stitch through all layers immediately beside the tree, the car, and each hill. Use a regular presser foot, a walking foot, or free-motion stitching for the quilting; work in the method with which you're most comfortable. To further highlight the shape of the hills and hold the quilt together, quilt a few lines in each hill, parallel to the curved hilltop. Vary the lines' length and spacing. Quilt along the hills within the landscape print or around the clouds or other shapes in an alternate background fabric.

19 Trim the batting and backing to match the quilt top. Cut 4 strips 2" (5 cm) wide across the width of the binding fabric and join into a continuous length (see Diagonal Seams for Joining Strips in Sewing Basics). Press the binding in half, lengthwise, with wrong sides together. Follow the instructions under Binding with Mitered Corners, option B, in Sewing Basics to bind the quilt edges. 🍃

- - - - - - - - - - - - - - - - - - -

KEVIN KOSBAB is a writer, an editor, and a pattern designer. His modern quilts and sewing projects have appeared in *Stitch* and *American Patchwork & Quilting,* and his Feed Dog Designs patterns are available on his website at feeddog.net.

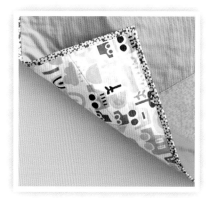

Hilltop Drive Baby Quilt
Tree

reversed for tracing

Enlarge templates on this page 150%

Hilltop Drive Baby Quilt
Car

**Enlarge templates on
this page 300%**

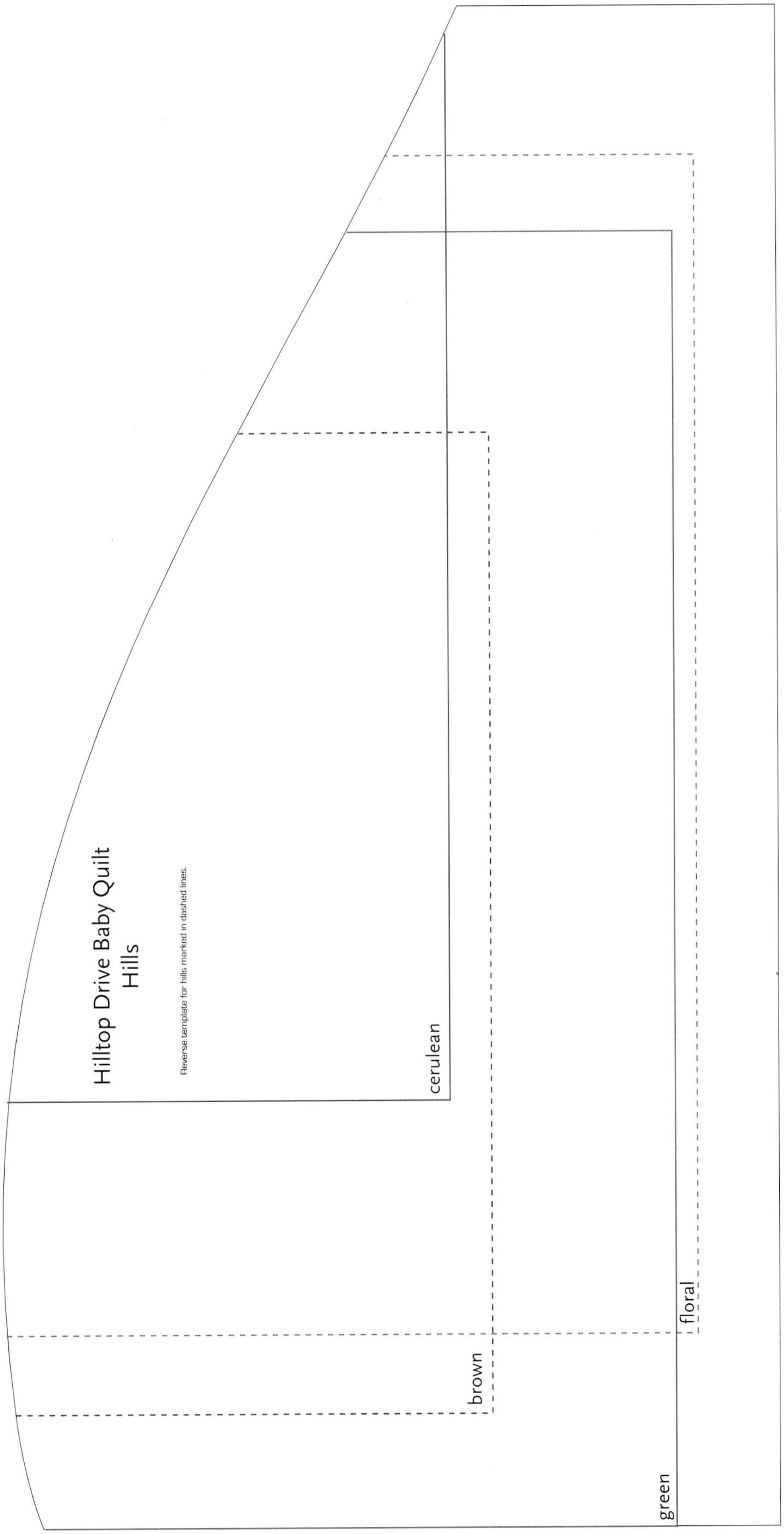

Hilltop Drive Baby Quilt
Hills

Reverse template for hills marked in dashed lines.

cerulean

floral

brown

green

Quilted Projects for You and Your Home

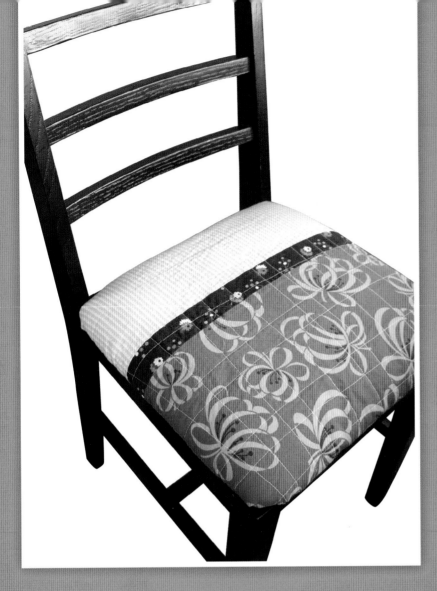

Quilted Seat Cushion

BY ANGELA PINGEL

If you have ever re-covered a seat cushion, you know that it is one of the least intimidating yet most rewarding ways to change a piece of furniture. Here is a unique method to create a quilted cover you can use to reupholster your chair.

Materials

☐ 3 pieces of fabric (see Step 1 to calculate amount of fabric needed)

☐ Flannel or lightweight batting

☐ Basting spray

☐ Chair to cover

☐ Staple gun

Directions

1 To determine the amount of fabric needed take the total dimension of the seat, front to back, and divide it into thirds. A medium-scale print is used in the top third of the seat cover, a strip of a small-scale print is used next, and a large-scale print is used as the focal fabric at the front of the chair. Add 5" (12.5 cm) to your measurements, all around, to allow for wrapping the fabric to the back and any shrinkage.

2 Using a ¼" (6 mm) seam allowance, sew the 3 pieces together.

3 Cut a piece of flannel (or lightweight batting) slightly larger than your patchwork fabric. Spray baste the flannel to the wrong side of the pieced fabric.

4 Mark straight, randomly angled lines across the fabric in 1 direction. Sew along these lines using a large stitch length and a contrasting color thread.

5 Turn the fabric 90 degrees and repeat Step 4.

6 Place the quilted fabric in the washer and dryer to achieve a crinkly cover.

7 Center the cover on the seat. Pull the excess fabric on 1 side to the back, pulling taut, and staple it in place. Do the same on the other side, and then the top and bottom. 🌿

- -

ANGELA PINGEL is a self-taught quilter. Her work can be seen in a number of publications, including *Modern Patchwork* and *101 Patchwork Projects + Quilts*. Visit her blog: cuttopieces.blogspot.com.

- -

Improv Scarf

BY ALISSA HAIGHT CARLTON

This modern scarf adds a fun pop of color to any outfit. A great project for learning basic improvisational piecing, it sews up in no time. It makes a great gift, and each one is unique!

Materials

- ☐ ⅝ yd (57.5 cm) of 45" (114.5 cm) wide woven fabric for scarf front, backing fabric #1, and patchwork (Main; shown: gray solid)

- ☐ ¼ yd (23 cm) of 45" (114.5 cm) wide woven fabric for backing fabric #2 and patchwork (Contrast A; shown: tweedy gray)

- ☐ Four 5" × 6" (12.5 × 15 cm) rectangles of woven fabrics for improvisationally pieced patchwork panel (shown: two grays, golden yellow, and teal; use the Main and Contrast A fabrics if desired)

- ☐ ⅜ yd (34.5 cm) of 45" (114.5 cm) wide flannel for interlining

- ☐ Piecing and quilting threads to match Main fabric

- ☐ Safety pins or quilter's basting pins

- ☐ Rotary cutter, rigid acrylic ruler, and self-healing mat

Finished Size

78" × 4" (198 × 10 cm)

Notes

* Seam allowances are ¼" (6 mm) unless otherwise noted.

* For explanations of terms and techniques, see Sewing Basics.

* Quilt batting can make the scarf stiff, so use flannel instead.

* If desired, substitute a flannel sheet for the flannel "batting" and cut one continuous 78½" × 5" (199 × 12.5 cm) strip.

* For small piecing as seen on the scarf, press seams open for a flat appearance.

Cut the Fabric

1 From the Main fabric, cut four strips 5" (12.5 cm) × the width of the fabric. Remove the selvedges and sew the strips together along the short ends to make a continuous strip; press the seams open. Cut the long strip into two pieces, one 70½" × 5" (179 × 12.5 cm) for scarf front and one 68½" × 5" (174 × 12.5 cm) for backing #1. Cut one 5" × 6" (12.5 × 15 cm) rectangle (patchwork) from the remaining strip.

2 From Contrast A, cut one 10½" × 5" (26.5 × 12.5 cm) rectangle for backing #2 and one 5" × 6" (12.5 × 15 cm) rectangle for patchwork.

3 From the flannel, cut two strips 5" (12.5 cm) × the width of the fabric. Remove the selvedges and sew the strips together along the short ends to make a continuous strip; press the seams open. Trim the strip to measure 78½" × 5" (199 × 12.5 cm).

Make the Patchwork Panel

Work with the four 5" × 6" (12.5 × 15 cm) rectangles.

4 Stack the 5" × 6" (12.5 × 15 cm) rectangles and, without using a ruler, cut each rectangle into four strips of varied widths (shown: roughly ¾"–1½" [1.9–3.8 cm] widths; **FIGURE 1**).

cut   cut   cut

figure 1

5 Arrange the strips into two sets of eight strips. Make each set unique, with random strip placement, for best contrast in the assembled patchwork (**FIGURE 2**).

6 With right sides together, sew the first two strips in the first set along one long edge. Add the third strip to the first two, and continue until the entire set is assembled. Press the seam allowances open. Repeat to join the second strip set. Because the strips were cut without a ruler, the edges may not align perfectly. This creates the improvisational look of the piecing; just be sure to use at least a ¼" (6 mm) seam allowance on each piece for secure seams. If desired, trim the seam allowances to ¼" (6 mm) after sewing.

7 Stack the assembled strip sets (**FIGURE 3**). Again working with no ruler, cut into three strips, cutting perpendicular to the seams. Vary the strip widths from roughly 1½ to 2" (3.8 to 5 cm).

figure 2

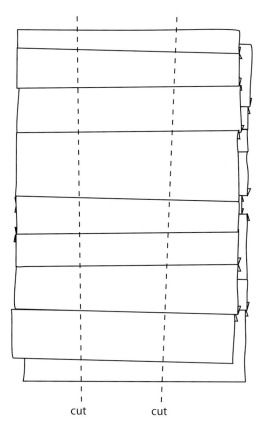

cut   cut

figure 3

8 Arrange the strips for a pleasing distribution of the different fabrics (**FIGURE 4**) and sew together as in Step 6. Press the seams open.

9 Using a ruler, square up and trim the finished patchwork panel to measure 8½" × 5" (21.5 × 12.5 cm).

Assemble the Scarf

10 Sew the patchwork panel to one short end of the 70½" × 5" (179 × 12.5 cm) Main fabric scarf front to create a 78½" × 5" (199 × 12.5 cm) strip. Press the seam open.

11 Sew backing pieces #1 and #2 together along one short edge and press the seam open.

12 Lay the scarf backing right-side up on a flat surface. Align the scarf front, wrong-side up, on the backing, matching the raw edges. Position the patchwork panel and the backing #2 panel at opposite ends of the scarf. Top with the flannel interlining.

13 Carefully align and pin all three layers along both long edges and the short end with the patchwork panel.

14 Using a ½" (1.3 cm) seam allowance, sew the three pinned edges, leaving the short end opposite the patchwork panel open for turning.

15 Trim the corners diagonally and turn the scarf right-side out. Use a point turner or other tool to work the corners into crisp points.

16 Press the entire scarf carefully so it lies flat. Turn ½" (1.3 cm) to the wrong side along the scarf's open end and press.

17 Use safety pins to baste all three layers together, working down the length of the scarf from the closed end. Adjust the pressed edges at the open end if necessary to ensure proper alignment of the front and back edges.

18 To quilt, sew ten lines of straight stitches close together in a band about 1" (2.5 cm) wide, positioning the quilting parallel to the long edges and to the left of the scarf's centerline. Begin and end the lines of quilting ½" (1.3 cm) from the scarf's short ends, backtacking to secure the stitches.

19 Edgestitch ⅛" (3 mm) from the scarf edges, closing the open end as you go. Enjoy your finished scarf! 🖋

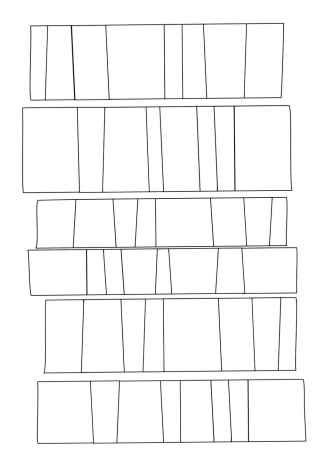

figure 4

ALISSA HAIGHT CARLTON is an avid quilter. She is one of the founders of the Modern Quilt Guild and co-author of the book *Block Party*. Visit her website at handmadebyalissa.com.

Patchwork Desk Set

BY LATIFAH SAAFIR

Brighten up your desk with a fun, quick, and easy project that you can make using just one 18" (45.5 cm) quilt block. This pattern uses a simple improv log cabin block, but you could use almost any block—either improv or not.

Materials

☐ 15 different colors of 2"–3" (5–7.5 cm) wide strips of fabric up to 18" (45.5 cm) long

☐ Template paper

☐ 18" (45.5 cm) square batting

☐ ½ yd (45.5 cm) backing fabric

☐ 1 magazine file

☐ 1 mini letter holder

☐ 1 round pencil cup (with the same diameter at the top and bottom)

☐ 1 desk pad calendar

Create Templates

1 **Magazine file and letter holder:** Trace the front of the magazine file and letter holder onto template paper. Add ¼" (6 mm) seam allowance on each side. Cut out.

2 **Pencil cup:** Measure the height of the pencil cup. Measure the diameter of the cup. Add ½" (1.3 cm) to each side for seam allowances. Cut out.

3 **Desk pad calendar:** Measure the width of the desk pad calendar adding ½" (1.3 cm) for seam allowances. Decide how far you would like the cover to come down on your desk pad calendar. Add ½" (1.3 cm) for seam allowances. Cut out.

Create Block

4 Using fabric strips, create one 18" (45.5 cm) log cabin block.

5 Layer the log cabin block right-side up on top of the batting and baste.

6 Machine quilt the block.

7 Pin the templates to the quilted log cabin block and cut out.

Create Magazine File, Letter Holder, and Desk Pad Calendar

8 From the backing fabric, cut 2 each of the magazine file, letter holder, and desk pad calendar templates.

9 Sew a hem on the bottom edge of 1 of the backing fabric pieces of the letter holder and desk pad calendar.

10 For the magazine file piece, sew a hem on the bottom and the 2 adjacent sides of 1 of the backing pieces. This will serve as the flap.

11 For the magazine file, layer the front (right-side up), the flap (right-side down), and the backing (right-side down). Pin all around, making sure not to catch the hemmed sides. Sew around the perimeter leaving 2" (5 cm) open for turning. Turn right-side out. Press. Whipstitch the turning hole closed.

12 Repeat Steps 7 and 8 for the desk pad calendar and letter holder.

Create Pencil Cup

13 Use the pencil cup template to cut out a backing fabric piece.

14 Layer the front and back right sides together. Sew the top and bottom edges together. Turn right-side out. Press.

15 Match 2 short sides together with the front sides facing. Being careful not to catch the backing, sew just the front sides together. Whipstitch the backing closed. Turn right-side out. 🖋

- -

Visit LATIFAH SAAFIR'S website at thequiltengineer.com.

Fabulous Floor Pillow

BY KAY WHITT

This quilted pillow with pretty scalloped edging is perfect for lounging on the floor in style. Five coordinating prints make a bold statement, and the fabric-covered buttons and scalloped back closure are the perfect finishing details.

Materials

Fabric requirements for A–E are based on 44" (112 cm) wide fabric.

☐ Fabric A: 1¼ yd (1.2 m) for pillow front and back

☐ Fabric B: 1 yd (91.5 cm) for pillow front and back

☐ Fabric C: 1 fat quarter or ½ yd (46 cm) for pillow front

☐ Fabric D: 1 fat quarter or ½ yd (46 cm) for pillow front

☐ Fabric E: 1¼ yd (1.2 m) for scalloped border

☐ 1½ yd (1.4 m) fusible fleece (Pellon Thermolam Plus recommended, TP971F)

☐ Small scrap of lightweight fusible interfacing (at least 3" × 9" [7.5 × 23 cm] or enough to cut 4 of the coverable button templates)

☐ 22" (56 cm) or 24" (61 cm) square pillow insert (use a 22" [56 cm] insert for a softer, flatter result; use a 24" [61 cm] for an overstuffed appearance as shown)

☐ Four 1½" (3.8 cm) wide coverable buttons (Maxant brand recommended)

☐ Matching sewing thread

☐ Rotary cutter and self-healing mat

☐ Chalk pencil

☐ Scallop templates on page 38

☐ Freezer paper to make scallop templates

☐ Buttonhole foot for your sewing machine

☐ Handsewing needle

Finished Size

26½" × 26½" (67.5 × 67.5 cm)

Note

✻ All seam allowances are ½" (1.3 cm) unless otherwise indicated.

Create Pillow Front

1 Cut a 12" (30.5 cm) square from each fabric, A–D **(FIGURE 1)**.

2 To form two rectangles, place the top two squares (A and B) right sides together and sew along the short edge, then press the seam allowances toward the darker fabric. Repeat with the bottom two fabrics (C and D).

3 Place the top and bottom sets of squares with right sides together to form one large square, being sure to match up the seams so they are even, then sew together. Press seam allowances to one side.

4 With the right side of the large square facing, mark ½" (1.3 cm) across the edge from one corner, then mark ½" (1.3 cm) down the opposite edge from the same corner. Repeat for each of the remaining three corners.

5 Cut four strips from fabric E, each measuring 33" × 5" (84 × 2.5 cm). Fold each strip in half widthwise to find the center of the strip and mark. With right sides together, pin each strip to one of the sides of the large square, matching up the center mark on each strip to the seam on each side of the large square and matching up the edges. **Note:** There will be excess strip that will extend on each end. Do not cut away, because this will be used for mitering the corners in the coming steps.

6 Starting at one of the ½" (1.3 cm) markings, begin sewing the strip to the large square, stopping when you reach the other ½" (⅓ cm) mark. Repeat for the remaining three strips. Flip the border strips to the outside of the large square and press flat.

7 To miter the corners, fold the large square in half, right sides together, diagonally from one of the corners. This will align the border strips so that they lie on top of each other right sides together. Be sure that the strips lie with raw edges evenly matched up.

8 At one of the corners near the diagonal fold, fold the top border strip upward at a 45-degree angle, starting at the corner of the pillow and extending away from the pillow itself **(FIGURE 2)**. Press this fold to create a crease.

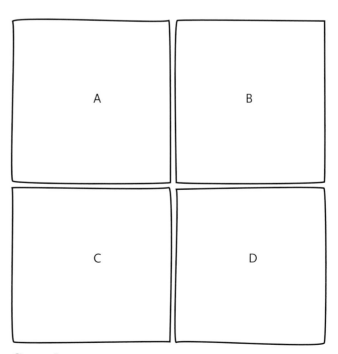

figure 1

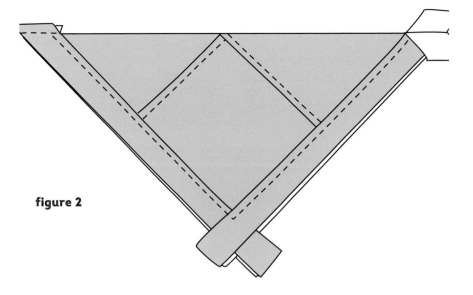

figure 2

9 After pressing the fold, lay the strip back down directly on top of the strip beneath it, right sides together, and open out the fold. Pin the strips together at the pressed crease. The crease will be the stitching line for mitering.

10 Repeat Steps 8 and 9 to miter the opposite corner along the same diagonal fold.

11 Repeat Step 7, folding so that the other two corners meet, then repeat Steps 8 and 9 to miter the two remaining corners.

12 Sew along each crease, starting at the corner of the pillow front where the strips come together and stitching outward to the edge of the strips (**FIGURE 2** shows the miter stitching line). Trim away the excess strip of fabric to within ½" (1.3 cm) of the seam and press the seam allowances open at each corner. Press the seam allowances at the border away from the large square.

13 Cut a piece of fusible fleece measuring 31" × 31" (79 × 79 cm). Lay the completed pillow front on top of the fusible side (bumpy or rough to the touch) of the fleece, with the right side facing up. Following the manufacturer's instructions, fuse the fleece to the pillow top. Trim away any excess fleece that may

remain beyond the raw edge of the pillow front fabric.

Create Scallop Border

14 Trace the Outer Edges Scallop Border pattern template onto the matte (non-waxy) side of the freezer paper, placing it on the fold as indicated and copying all guidelines and markings; be sure to notch the center point (on the fold). Cut out. Align the template along one of the borders, with the straight edge of the template lying along the seam attaching the border to the large square; match the center seam of the squares to the center marking on the template and the angled edges to the mitered seams. *Note: Due to the differences from one sewer to the next, slight adjustments may need to be made depending on how accurate the seams were completed. Make any adjustments necessary to get the scallop template to align properly.*

15 Iron the freezer-paper template to the border with the shiny side of the paper against the right side of the fabric. This will cause a temporary bond of the pattern piece to the fabric so that the scallops can be traced. Trace around the scalloped edges with a chalk pencil. Peel away the paper, iron to a new side, and repeat the tracing process until all

edges of the border have been marked. Trim along the scalloped edge markings, cutting through all layers.

16 Topstitch directly on top of the seams attaching the small squares to each other (stitching on top of an existing seam is called "stitching in the ditch") to secure the fleece to the pillow front. Do not stitch in the ditch where the border and squares meet because this stitching will occur in a later step. Set the pillow front aside.

Create Pillow Back

17 From fabric A, cut two rectangles for the top back panel, each measuring 15" × 23" (38 × 58.5 cm). If the pattern of the fabric is directional, make sure that it runs in the correct direction along the 15" (38 cm) width. Cut a piece of fusible fleece also measuring 15" × 23" (38 × 58.5 cm).

18 Fuse the fleece to the wrong side of one of the fabric A pieces just cut.

19 Trace the Back Scallop Border Template onto the matte side of the freezer paper and cut out as in Step 14.

20 On the back panel with the fleece attached, align the template with one of the 23" (58.5 cm) sides (center the template between the ½" [1.3 cm] seam

figure 3

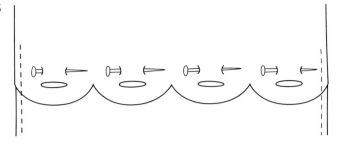

allowances on each side). Iron the paper in place along the edge so that the top of the scallops lines up with the outer edge of the fabric; trace the scallops with a chalk pencil. Remove the paper and cut out the scallops.

21 Place the scalloped back panel on top of the other back panel with right sides together, lining up the raw edges. Pin along the scalloped edge only. Using a ¼" (6 mm) seam allowance and with the scalloped back panel facing up, stitch the two pieces together along the curves of the scallops. Trim away the excess fabric so that the edges of both panels match (follow the scalloped edge) and then clip along the curves of the scallops by cutting small triangles into the seam allowances with the point of the triangles facing the seam. Cut close to the seam line, but be careful not to cut into it. This will ensure that the piece will lie flat without puckering when turned.

22 Turn the scallops right-side out and use your fingers to smooth out the curves. Press the scalloped edge so that the curves are well defined and the seam is flat. Be careful in your pressing so that the fabric from the other side of the scallop does not show. Realign the three remaining raw edges and pin in place.

23 With the right side of the piece with the fleece attached facing up, begin topstitching along the curves of the scallops ¼" (6 mm) away from the finished edge. Continue stitching along the three remaining raw edges, about ⅜" (1 cm) from the raw edges.

24 Choose one or more of the fabrics (A–D) to make the covered buttons. Using the template provided by the coverable button manufacturer, cut four circles from the interfacing scrap. Place these interfacing circles on the wrong side of the fabrics chosen for

the buttons and fuse in place according to manufacturer's instructions. Cut out the circles from the fabric(s). Follow the instructions on the button package to complete the buttons using the circles to cover them. Note: The purpose of the interfacing is to give the fabric additional thickness so that the shiny metal of the button form does not show through the fabric.

25 On the right side of the scalloped back panel (the side with the fleece attached) measure in 1¾" (4.5 cm) from the center of the edge of each scallop and mark. Draw a guideline with the

chalk pencil through each mark for a centered (top to the bottom of the scallop) 1¾" (4.5 cm) buttonhole that runs parallel to the edge **(FIGURE 3)**. With the buttonhole foot on the sewing machine, sew buttonholes over each guideline. Clip open the buttonholes between the two lines of stitching. Set this piece aside.

26 For the bottom back panel of the pillow, cut a rectangle from fabric B measuring 29" × 23" (73.5 × 58.5 cm). If the fabric pattern is directional, have the pattern running in the correct direction along the 29" (73.5 cm) length. Fold the fabric in half with wrong sides together so that it measures 14½" × 23" (37 × 58.5 cm) and press the fold.

27 Cut a piece of fusible fleece that measures 14½" × 23" (37 × 58.5 cm). Unfold the back panel and place the fleece against the wrong side, with one edge of the fleece along the fold and the other fleece edges even with the remaining three edges. Fuse in

place according to the manufacturer's instructions.

28 Fold the back panel in half again along the existing fold so that the fleece is "sandwiched" between the layers of fabric. Align the raw edges and pin in place. Stitch around the outside raw edges, about ⅜" (1 cm) away from the edge. Topstitch along the folded edge ¼" (6 mm) from the edge.

29 Position the top back panel piece on the bottom back panel piece with right sides (with fleece attached) up so that the scalloped edge of the top panel overlaps the topstitched, folded edge of the bottom panel by about 3" (7.5 cm). Make sure that your button-holes are facing up. Pin the back panels together and measure from the top of one piece down to the other end. This piece should now measure about 23" (58.5 cm) square. If it is smaller or larger, adjust the amount of overlap between the two pieces until the correct measurement is achieved. Tack the lay-ers together by stitching them together on each side of the overlap, about ¼" (6 mm) from the edge (FIGURE 3).

30 Mark through the center of each buttonhole onto the lower fabric for button placement. Sew the buttons in place and then button the two sections together.

31 To add the border to the back panel, repeat Steps 5–12.

Assemble the Pillow Cover

32 Once the border has been added, unbutton the back panels and place the pillow front and pillow back right sides together with the outer edges even. Note that the back piece has straight edges and the front is scalloped. Pin the two pieces together.

33 Using a ¼" (6 mm) seam allowance and with the pillow front facing up, stitch the pieces together, following the curves of the scallops. Trim away the excess fabric so that the back piece matches the curves of the front piece, then clip along the curves as in Step 21 so that the seam will lie flat.

34 Turn the pillow cover right-side out through the back panel opening and use your fingers to smooth out the curves.

Press the pillow edges flat and smooth. Topstitch ¼" (6 mm) away from the finished edge, following the curves of the scallops.

35 Button the pillow cover closed and turn it over so that the front side is facing up. Pin the pillow cover together through all thicknesses along the border seam on all four sides. Topstitch on top of the border fabric about ¼" (6 mm) away from the seam, all the way around.

36 Unbutton the pillow cover and place the pillow insert inside. Button closed and enjoy! 🍃

- -

KAY WHITT launched Serendipity Gifts in 2001. She is a licensed designer who designs sewing patterns for clothing and accessories. Visit her website at sewserendipity.blogspot.com.

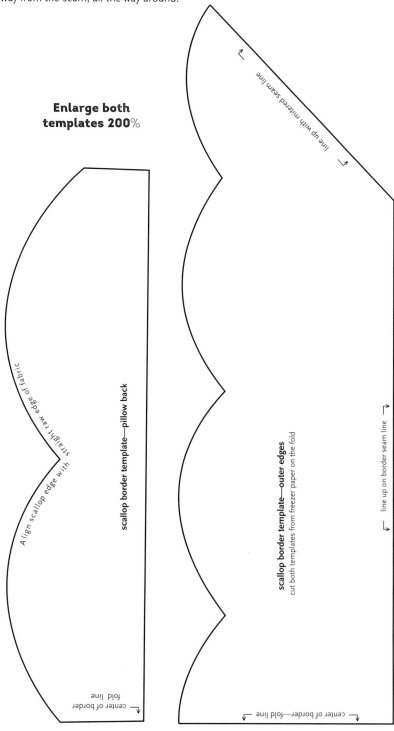

Enlarge both templates 200%

scallop border template—pillow back

Align scallop edge with straight raw edge of fabric

center of border—fold line

line up with mitered seam line

scallop border template—outer edges
cut both templates from freezer paper on the fold

line up on border seam line

center of border—fold line

Patchwork Quilted Belt

BY BARI J. ACKERMAN

Here's a great project for using up all your little scraps. Don't worry about patterns and colors; feel free to mix it up. The more random, the more unique the finished product. The belts shown here feature fabrics from my debut collection, Full Bloom for Windham Fabrics.

Materials

☐ Sewing machine

☐ A variety of scrap fabrics (at least
4" [10 cm] wide pieces)

☐ Matching thread

☐ Fusible fleece

☐ Belt buckle

Directions

1 Cut strips from a variety of fabrics. To figure out how wide the strips should be, multiply the width of your buckle opening by 2, and add ½" (1.3 cm). (I used a buckle with a 1½" opening, so I cut my fabrics 3½" [9 cm] wide.) Cut fabric pieces in various lengths, with the total length adding up to about 1½ yd (1.3 m).

2 Using a ¼" (6 mm) seam allowance, stitch the pieces together in a random order to make a strip. The finished strip should be about 3½" (9 cm) longer than the desired length of the completed belt. Press the seams open.

3 Cut a piece of fusible fleece that is the same width and length as your pieced fabric strip.

4 Press the fusible fleece onto the wrong side of the fabric.

5 Make a ¼" (6 mm) fold toward the wrong side at each end of your belt, and press in place.

6 Fold your belt in half lengthwise, with right sides facing. Match the seams and pin.

7 Sew along the long side using a ¼" (6 mm) seam allowance to create an inside-out tube. Turn the tube right-side out and press it flat with the seam centered along the back side of the belt.

8 Fold each corner at one end of the belt into a 45-degree triangle toward the seam side of the belt. Stitch across the base of the triangle and then topstitch ⅛" (3 mm) from the edge of the belt all the way down one side. Just before you get to the other end of the belt, fold each corner into the shape of a triangle, as before. With your needle down, turn to sew across the base of the triangle and then sew along the other edge, as

you did before, until you reach the place you started. Topstitch along the triangle shape to finish that end.

9 Topstitch or quilt a decorative curvy line to the other end and back again.

10 Measure the desired length for your belt. At that length, fold the excess toward the seam side of your belt and attach the buckle, making sure it will be facing the correct side when you are finished. Topstitch the triangle you created on the end to hold in place. 🖋

- -

BARI J. ACKERMAN is a product/textile designer. She designs limited-edition handbags and accessories, and she has a line of sewing patterns called Keeping it Real. Bari is the author of *Inspired to Sew*. Visit her online at barijonline.com.

Tip
- - - - - - - - - - - - - -
+ You'll have more control of the fabric if you press on the fabric side as opposed to the fleece side.

Easy Quilted Pot Holders
Using String Piecing

BY ASHLEY NEWCOMB

Add a little color to your kitchen with these bright and cheerful pot holders! Use a variety of fabric scraps for a colorful set, or select several fabrics in a single shade to coordinate with your kitchen. The pot holder patchwork is pieced using a simple paper foundation technique—it's a fun method to try if you've never used it.

Materials

For 2 pot holders

☐ A selection of print fabric scraps, cut into strips about 1"–1½" × 7½" (2.5–3.8 × 19 cm) or less

☐ White fabric, 8 strips 1" × 8" (2.5 × 20.5 cm)

☐ Copy paper, 8 squares 5" × 5" (12.5 × 12.5 cm)

☐ Backing fabric, 2 squares 9½" × 9½" (24 × 24 cm)

☐ Cotton quilt batting, 2 squares 9½" × 9½" (24 × 24 cm)

☐ Insul-Bright, 2 squares 9½" × 9½" (24 × 24 cm)

☐ Binding fabric, 2 strips 2½" × 42" (6.5 × 106.5 cm)

☐ Fabric for the hanging loops, 1 piece 2" × 12" (5 × 30.5 cm)

☐ Glue stick (Select one that is safe for fabric use.)

Finished Size

9" × 9" (23 × 23 cm)

Directions

1 Fold a 5" (12.5 cm) square of copy paper in half diagonally to mark the diagonal; open the square. Using the glue stick, apply a thin line of glue along the diagonal. Attach a 1" (2.5 cm) strip of white fabric along this line, making sure to center it along the diagonal line. Repeat this step for each of the 7 remaining 5" (12.5 cm) squares.

2 Align 1 of the printed fabric strips along the edge of the white strip, right sides together. Make sure your fabric strip is long enough to cover the paper square. Sew along this line using a ¼" (6 mm) seam allowance.

3 Press the fabric strip open with a dry iron or finger-press it.

4 Repeat Steps 2–3, aligning the next fabric strip with the strip you just added. Continue until 1 side of the paper square is entirely covered. Then repeat the process to add strips to cover the other half of the paper square.

5 Flip the square over and trim the block, using the paper square as your guide.

6 Repeat Steps 2–5 for the remaining 7 blocks. Remove the paper backing by folding the paper along the stitch lines and tearing it away.

7 Using 4 blocks for each pot holder, arrange them in 2 rows of 2 blocks. Sew the blocks in each row together, and then sew the rows together, resulting in two 9½" (24 cm) squares.

8 Stack the layers for each pot holder in the following order: string pot holder top (right-side up), quilt batting, Insul-Bright, backing (right-side down).

9 Baste and quilt as desired.

10 To make the 2 hanging loops, fold and press the 2" × 12" (5 × 30.5 cm) piece of fabric in half lengthwise, wrong sides together. Then open the strip and turn each long edge in to meet the fold line; press. Fold in half and press again,

Tip

+ Reduce your stitch length so you'll be able to remove the paper backing later on. A stitch length of about 1.5 mm works well.

Tip

+ Use a fun piece of selvedge as your hanging loop—only one edge needs to be hemmed!

enclosing the edges. Stitch along the length ⅛" (3 mm) from the edge and then cut in half, resulting in 2 pieces, each 6" (15 cm) in length.

11 Trim each pot holder to 9" × 9" (23 × 23 cm) square. To attach the hanging loops, fold each 6" (15 cm) loop in half and sew to the pot holder backing about 1" (2.5 cm) from the top corner.

12 Make and attach the binding, following your desired binding method. 🌿

ASHLEY NEWCOMB creates modern patchwork-style quilts. She likes to mix and match great fabrics and and uses improvisational piecing. See more of her work at filminthefridge.com.

Sewing Basics

A quick reference guide to basic tools, techniques, and terms

For all projects (unless otherwise indicated):

✻ When piecing: Use ¼" (6 mm) seam allowances. Stitch with the right sides together. After stitching a seam, press it to set the seam; then open the fabrics and press the seam allowance toward the darker fabric.

✻ Yardages are based upon 44" (112 cm) wide fabric.

Sewing Kit

The following items are essential for your sewing kit. Make sure you have these tools on hand before starting any of the projects:

✻ **ACRYLIC RULER** This is a clear flat ruler, with a measuring grid at least 2" × 18" (5 × 45.5 cm). A rigid acrylic (quilter's) ruler should be used when working with a rotary cutter. You should have a variety of rulers in different shapes and sizes.

✻ **BATTING** 100% cotton, 100% wool, plus bamboo, silk, and blends.

✻ **BONE FOLDER** Allows you to make non-permanent creases in fabric, paper, and other materials.

✻ **CRAFT SCISSORS** To use when cutting out paper patterns.

✻ **EMBROIDERY SCISSORS** These small scissors are used to trim off threads, clip corners, and do other intricate cutting work.

✻ **FABRIC** Commercial prints, hand-dyes, cottons, upholstery, silks, wools; the greater the variety of types, colors, designs, and textures, the better.

✻ **FABRIC MARKING PENS/PENCILS + TAILOR'S CHALK** Available in several colors for use on light and dark fabrics; use to trace patterns and pattern markings onto your fabric. Tailor's chalk is available in triangular pieces, rollers, and pencils. Some forms (such as powdered) can simply be brushed away; refer to the manufacturer's instructions for the recommended removal method for your chosen marking tool.

✻ **FREE-MOTION OR DARNING FOOT** Used to free-motion quilt.

✻ **FUSIBLE WEB** Used to fuse fabrics together. There are a variety of products on the market.

✻ **GLUE** Glue stick, fabric glue, and all-purpose glue.

✻ **HANDSEWING + EMBROIDERY NEEDLES** Keep an assortment of sewing and embroidery needles in different sizes, from fine to sturdy.

✻ **IRON, IRONING BOARD + PRESS CLOTHS** An iron is an essential tool when sewing. Use cotton muslin or silk organza as a press cloth to protect delicate fabric surfaces from direct heat. Use a Teflon sheet or parchment paper to protect your iron and ironing board when working with fusible web.

✻ **MEASURING TAPE** Make sure it's at least 60" (152.5 cm) long and retractable.

✻ **NEEDLE THREADER** An inexpensive aid to make threading the eye of the needle superfast.

✻ **PINKING SHEARS** These shears have notched teeth that leave a zigzag edge on the cut cloth to prevent fraying.

✻ **POINT TURNER** A blunt, pointed tool that helps push out the corners of a project and/or smooth seams. A knitting needle or chopstick may also be used.

✻ **ROTARY CUTTER + SELF-HEALING MAT** Useful for cutting out fabric quickly. Always use a mat to protect the blade and your work surface (a rigid acrylic ruler should be used with a rotary cutter to make straight cuts).

✻ **SAFETY PINS** Always have a bunch on hand.

✻ **SCISSORS + SHEARS** Heavy-duty shears reserved for fabric only; a pair of small, sharp embroidery scissors; thread snips; a pair of all-purpose scissors; pinking shears.

✻ **SEAM RIPPER** Handy for quickly ripping out stitches.

✻ **SEWING MACHINE** With free-motion capabilities.

✻ **STRAIGHT PINS + PINCUSHION** Always keep lots of pins nearby.

✻ **TEMPLATE SUPPLIES** Keep freezer paper or other large paper (such as parchment paper) on hand for tracing the templates you intend to use. Regular office paper may be used for templates that will fit. You should also have card stock or plastic if you wish to make permanent templates that can be reused.

✻ **THIMBLE** Your fingers and thumbs will thank you.

✻ **THREAD** All types, including hand and machine thread for stitching and quilting; variegated; metallic; 100% cotton; monofilament.

✻ **ZIPPER FOOT** An accessory foot for your machine with a narrow profile that can be positioned to sew close to the zipper teeth. A zipper foot is adjustable so the foot can be moved to either side of the needle.

Glossary of Sewing Terms and Techniques

BACKSTITCH Stitching in reverse for a short distance at the beginning and end of a seam line to secure the stitches. Most machines have a button or knob for this function (also called backtack).

BASTING Using long, loose stitches to hold something in place temporarily. To baste by machine, use the longest straight stitch length available on your machine. To baste by hand, use stitches at least ¼" (6 mm) long. Use a contrasting thread to make the stitches easier to spot for removal.

BIAS The direction across a fabric that is located at a 45-degree angle from the lengthwise or crosswise grain. The bias has high stretch and a very fluid drape.

BIAS TAPE Made from fabric strips cut on a 45-degree angle to the grainline, the bias cut creates an edging fabric that will stretch to enclose smooth or curved edges. You can buy bias tape ready-made or make your own.

CLIPPING CURVES Involves cutting tiny slits or triangles into the seam allowance of curved edges so the seam will lie flat when turned right-side out. Cut slits along concave curves and triangles (with points toward the seam line) along a convex curve. Be careful not to clip into the stitches.

CLIP THE CORNERS Clipping the corners of a project reduces bulk and allows for crisper corners in the finished project. To clip a corner, cut off a triangle-shaped piece of fabric across the seam allowances at the corner. Cut close to the seam line but be careful not to cut through the stitches.

DART This stitched triangular fold is used to give shape and form to the fabric to fit body curves.

EDGESTITCH A row of topstitching placed very close (¹⁄₁₆"–⅛" [2–3 mm]) to an edge or an existing seam line.

FABRIC GRAIN The grain is created in a woven fabric by the threads that travel lengthwise and crosswise. The lengthwise grain runs parallel to the selvedges; the crosswise grain should always be perpendicular to the lengthwise threads. If the grains aren't completely straight and perpendicular, grasp the fabric at diagonally opposite corners and pull gently to restore the grain. In knit fabrics, the lengthwise grain runs along the wales (ribs), parallel to the selvedges, with the crosswise grain running along the courses (perpendicular to the wales).

FINGER-PRESS Pressing a fold or crease with your fingers as opposed to using an iron.

FUSSY-CUT Cutting a specific motif from a commercial or hand-printed fabric. Generally used to center a motif in a patchwork pattern or to feature a specific motif in an appliqué design. Use a clear acrylic ruler or template plastic to isolate the selected motif and ensure that it will fit within the desired size, including seam allowances.

GRAINLINE A pattern marking showing the direction of the grain. Make sure the grainline marked on the pattern runs parallel to the lengthwise grain of your fabric, unless the grainline is specifically marked as crosswise or bias.

INTERFACING Material used to stabilize or reinforce fabrics. Fusible interfacing has an adhesive coating on one side that adheres to fabric when ironed.

LINING The inner fabric of a garment or bag, used to create a finished interior that covers the raw edges of the seams.

MITER Joining a seam or fold at an angle that bisects the project corner. Most common is a 45-degree angle, like a picture frame, but shapes other than squares or rectangles will have miters with different angles.

OVERCAST STITCH A machine stitch that wraps around the fabric raw edge to finish edges and prevent unraveling. Some sewing machines have several overcast stitch options; consult your sewing machine manual for information on stitch settings and the appropriate presser foot for the chosen stitch (often the standard presser foot can be used). A zigzag stitch can be used as an alternative to finish raw edges if your machine doesn't have an overcast stitch function.

PRESHRINK Many fabrics shrink when washed; you need to wash, dry, and press all your fabric before you start to sew, following the suggested cleaning method marked on the fabric bolt (keep in mind that the appropriate cleaning method may not be machine washing). Don't skip this step!

RIGHT SIDE The front side, or the side that should be on the outside of a finished garment. On a print fabric, the print will be stronger on the right side of the fabric.

RIGHT SIDES TOGETHER The right sides of two fabric layers should be facing each other.

SATIN STITCH (MACHINE) This is a smooth, completely filled column of zig-zag stitches achieved by setting the stitch length short enough for complete coverage but long enough to prevent bunching and thread buildup.

SEAM ALLOWANCE The amount of fabric between the raw edge and the seam.

SELVEDGE This is the tightly woven border on the lengthwise edges of woven fabric and the finished lengthwise edges of knit fabric.

SQUARING UP After you have pieced together a fabric block or section, check to make sure the edges are straight and the measurements are correct. Use a rotary cutter and an acrylic ruler to trim the block if necessary.

STITCH IN THE DITCH Lay the quilt sandwich right-side up under the presser foot and sew along the seam line "ditch." The stitches will fall between the two fabric pieces and disappear into the seam.

TOPSTITCH Used to hold pieces firmly in place and/or to add a decorative effect, a topstitch is simply a stitch that can be seen on the outside of the garment or piece. To topstitch, make a line of stitching on the outside (right side) of the piece, usually a set distance from an existing seam.

UNDERSTITCHING A line of stitches placed on a facing (or lining), very near the facing/garment seam. Understitching is used to hold the seam allowances and facing together and to prevent the facing from rolling toward the outside of the garment.

WRONG SIDE The wrong side of the fabric is the underside, or the side that should be on the inside of a finished garment. On a print fabric, the print will be lighter or less obvious on the wrong side of the fabric.

Stitch Glossary

BACKSTITCH

Working from right to left, bring the needle up at **1** and insert behind the starting point at **2**. Bring the needle up at **3**; repeat by inserting at **1** and bringing the needle up at a point that is a stitch length beyond **3**.

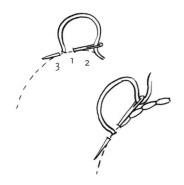

BASTING STITCH

Using the longest straight stitch length on your machine, baste to temporarily hold fabric layers and seams in position for final stitching. It can also be done by hand. When basting, use a contrasting thread to make it easier to spot when you're taking it out.

BLANKET STITCH

Working from left to right, bring the needle up at **1** and insert at **2**. Bring the needle back up at **3** and over the working thread. Repeat by making the next stitch in the same manner, keeping the spacing even.

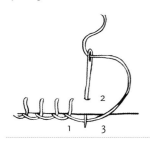

BLINDSTITCH/BLIND-HEM STITCH

Used mainly for hemming fabrics where an inconspicuous hem is difficult to achieve (this stitch is also useful for securing binding on the wrong side). Fold the hem edge back about ¼" (6 mm). Take a small stitch in the garment, picking up only a few threads of the fabric, then take the next stitch ¼" (6 mm) ahead in the hem. Continue, alternating stitches between the hem and the garment (if using for a non-hemming application, simply alternate stitches between the two fabric edges being joined).

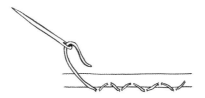

CHAIN STITCH

Working from top to bottom, bring the needle up at and reinsert at **1** to create a loop; do not pull the thread taut. Bring the needle back up at **2**, keeping the needle above the loop and gently pulling the needle toward you to tighten the loop flush to the fabric. Repeat by inserting the needle at **2** to form a loop and bring the needle up at **3**. Tack the last loop down with a straight stitch.

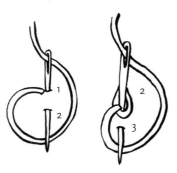

STRAIGHT STITCH + RUNNING STITCH

Working from right to left, make a straight stitch by bringing the needle up and insert at **1**, ⅛"–¼" (3–6 mm) from the starting point. To make a line of running stitches (a row of straight stitches worked one after the other), bring the needle up at **2** and repeat.

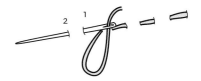

FRENCH KNOT

Bring the needle up at **1** and hold the thread taut above the fabric. Point the needle toward your fingers and move the needle in a circular motion to wrap the thread around the needle once or twice. Insert the needle near **1** and hold the thread taut near the knot as you pull the needle and thread through the knot and the fabric to complete.

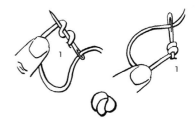

COUCHING

Working from right to left, use one thread, known as the couching or working thread, to tack down one or more strands of fiber, known as the couched fibers. Bring the working thread up at **1** and insert at **2**, over the fibers to tack them down, bringing the needle back up at **3**. The fibers are now encircled by the couching thread. Repeat to couch the desired length of fiber(s). This stitch may also be worked from left to right, and the spacing between the couching threads may vary for different design effects.

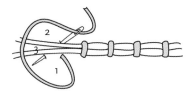

CROSS-STITCH

Working from right to left, bring the needle up at **1**, insert at **2**, then bring the needle back up at **3**. Finish by inserting the needle at **4**. Repeat for the desired number of stitches.

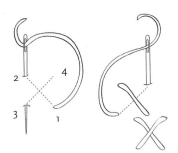

WHIPSTITCH

Bring the needle up at **1**, insert at **2**, and bring up at **3**. These quick stitches do not have to be very tight or close together.

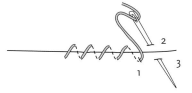

STANDARD HAND-APPLIQUÉ STITCH

Cut a length of thread 12"–18" (30.5–45.5 cm). Thread the newly cut end through the eye of the needle, pull this end through, and knot it. Use this technique to thread the needle and knot the thread to help keep the thread's "twist" intact and to reduce knotting. Beginning at the straightest edge of the appliqué and working from right to left, bring the needle up from the underside, through the background fabric and the very edge of the appliqué at **1**, catching only a few threads of the appliqué fabric. Pull the thread taut, then insert the needle into the background fabric at **2**, as close as possible to **1**. Bring the needle up through the background fabric at **3**, ⅛" (3 mm) beyond **2**. Continue in this manner, keeping the thread taut (do not pull it so tight that the fabric puckers) to keep the stitching as invisible as possible.

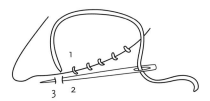

SLIP STITCH

Working from right to left, join two pieces of fabric by taking a ¹⁄₁₆"–¼" (2–6 mm) long stitch into the folded edge of one piece of fabric and bringing the needle out. Insert the needle into the folded edge of the other piece of fabric, directly across from the point where the thread emerged from the previous stitch. Repeat by inserting the needle into the first piece of fabric. The thread will be almost entirely hidden inside the folds of the fabrics.

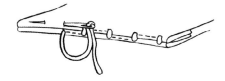

Create Binding

CUTTING STRAIGHT STRIPS

Cut strips on the crosswise grain, from selvedge to selvedge. Use a rotary cutter and straightedge to obtain a straight cut. Remove the selvedges and join the strips with diagonal seams (see instructions at right).

CUTTING BIAS STRIPS

Fold one cut end of the fabric to meet one selvedge, forming a fold at a 45-degree angle to the selvedge (1). With the fabric placed on a self-healing mat, cut off the fold with a rotary cutter, using a straightedge as a guide to make a straight cut. With the straightedge and rotary cutter, cut strips to the appropriate width (2). Join the strips with diagonal seams.

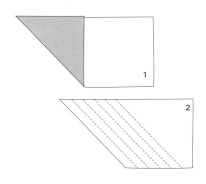

BINDING WITH MITERED CORNERS

Decide whether you will use a Double-fold Binding (option A at right) or a Double-layer Binding (option B at right). *If using double-layer binding follow the alternate italicized instructions in parenthesis.*

Open the binding and press ½" (1.3 cm) to the wrong side at one short end (*refold the binding at the center crease and proceed*). Starting with the folded-under end of the binding, place it near the center of the first edge of the project to be bound, matching the raw edges, and pin in place. Begin sewing near the center of one edge of the project, along the first crease (*at the appropriate distance from the raw edge*), leaving several inches of the binding fabric free at the beginning. Stop sewing ¼" (6 mm) before reaching the corner, backstitch, and cut the threads. Rotate the project 90 degrees to position it for sewing the next side. Fold the binding fabric up, away from the project, at a 45-degree angle (1), then fold it back

down along the project raw edge (2). This forms a miter at the corner. Stitch the second side, beginning at the project raw edge (2) and ending ¼" (6 mm) from the next corner, as before.

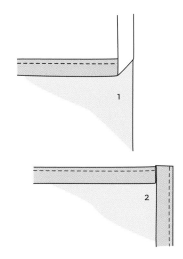

Continue as established until you have completed the last corner. Continue stitching until you are a few inches from the beginning edge of the binding fabric. Overlap the pressed beginning edge of the binding by ½" (1.3 cm) (or overlap more as necessary for security) and trim the working edge to fit. Finish sewing the binding (*opening the center fold and tucking the raw edge inside the pressed end of the binding strip*). Refold the binding along all the creases and then fold it over the project raw edges to the back, enclosing the raw edges (*there are no creases to worry about with option B*). The folded edge of the binding strip should just cover the stitches visible on the project back. Slip-stitch or blindstitch the binding in place, tucking in the corners to complete the miters as you go (3).

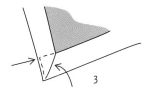

DIAGONAL SEAMS FOR JOINING STRIPS

Lay two strips right sides together, at right angles. The area where the strips overlap forms a square. Sew diagonally across the square as shown above. Trim the excess fabric ¼" (6 mm) away from the seam line and press the seam allowances open. Repeat to join all the strips, forming one long fabric band.

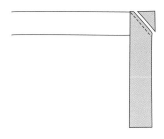

FOLD BINDING

A. Double-fold Binding

This option will create binding that is similar to packaged double-fold bias tape/binding. Fold the strip in half lengthwise, with wrong sides together; press. Open up the fold and then fold each long edge toward the wrong side, so that the raw edges meet in the middle (1). Refold the binding along the existing center crease, enclosing the raw edges (2), and press again.

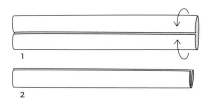

B. Double-layer Binding

This option creates a double-thick binding with only one fold. This binding is often favored by quilters. Fold the strip in half lengthwise with wrong sides together; press.

Find popular patterns for quick and easy projects with these *Craft Tree* publications, brought to you by Interweave.

Colorful Projects for Outdoor Fun
ISBN 978-1-62033-561-1

Easy Quilting Projects
ISBN 978-1-62033-556-7

Easy Sewing Projects
ISBN 978-1-62033-558-1

Great Projects for Guys
ISBN 978-1-62033-559-8

More Teacher Gifts
ISBN 978-1-62033-560-4

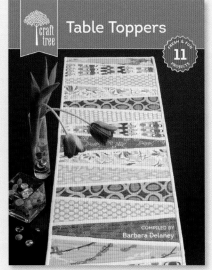

Table Toppers
ISBN 978-1-62033-557-4

Visit your favorite retailer or order online at interweavestore.com

INTERWEAVE.
interweavestore.com